Gentle Fragments

Peter Hawley

Presentation by *BookLeaf Publishing*

Web: www.bookleafpub.com

E-mail: info@bookleafpub.com

ISBN: 9789357613668

First edition 2022

PREFACE

In her Nobel lecture "The Tender Narrator," Polish writer Olga Tokarczuk states how "Life is created by events, but it is only when we are able to interpret them, try to understand them and lend them meaning that they are transformed into experience." I'd like to think of this small collection of poetry that I've put forth on these pages as an attempt in trying to make meaning of events - real and imagined - in my life. As my title suggests, I do not treat this collection as a finished product of any sort, but rather as a basic foundation for me to experiment, expand, or eventually abandon some of the poems found here as I continue to develop my skills as a writer. Further on in her lecture, Tokarczuk goes on to say that "Perhaps we should trust fragments, as it is fragments that create constellations capable of describing more, and in a more complex way, multi-dimensionally." It is with fragments, rather "gentle fragments" of the mind that help us build the way to more coherent lines of creative thinking.

Juggling

Let us return to Marisela Gonzalez
and consider she was juggling
as she faced an unfamiliar earthquake

and, storm.

As a result, she resorted to
their plight with sincere empathy.

The pressure of being.

Emanation

Slender beams of light enter
This darkened room as I kneel.
Always silent, always alone.
Frozen here.
Waiting.

Tortured forms wrought in panes of glass loom
as
Dust dances in the air.
Forming an image in my mind.
Searing my naked flesh.

The devout clutching at their rosaries.
Grasping at their earrings.

I discover paleness on a lover's face.
Disfigured and uncanny.
Familiar yet unbeknownst to human shapes.

Self-made martyrs are seen crying and yelling at
each other.
In the midst of a projected downturn.

A monster doing away with its enemies
As those enemies call it friend.

Stationed in a site for pilgrimage

Where an ancient form delivered in cloth,
Carried down for five generations,
Is centered around the crowded.
Waiting for its loved ones to return.

But the Gods keep themselves at a distance,
Finding fortune in the reluctant heroes.

I raise my head, now embracing
This callous truth.

Being Me

Though if I thrive and I am cast away
My edge will falter as I leave the room
That I might see what the old world could say
And sweets grown common lose their total
crume
I have a father and so will my son
And yet, in my own view, love will be rare
Receiving hate once everything is done
And much of my life is done on a dare
Over whom my friends walk with gentle gait
Without the danger or the true terror
Thus my life becomes my own a bit too late
I tried to avoid all of this in error
My pain, though delayed, must be true to me
Which in my heart, must be the place to be

Online Dating

Measure evenly the sights
The stars are bending and crying
My gratitude shows out for you
But my envy is like a mangled forest
Nerves and shears outside of my control

I love who you've met
As I eagerly search for those
who are also wanderers
Never staying too long in mind
with one place, even if they've
been nowhere else

Getting your point across
and finding someone who listens is like
guiding the universe towards you.

Inaction

Sever my mind to everything I am.
I want to preach above wings, above the sky.
Endless minds wish for me to do something.
Something about the leader, something about the
world.
I'm constantly disappointed as to how we really
look ...

Drama

Scare me into happiness.
Philosophy is for those who either think or don't.
Let's agree upon the fact that we are not truthful,
Staying silent even when we say we are
sociable.

Being cruel when we say we are friendly.
I spot my own inconsistencies as traits, not
flaws,
As I presume everyone else does.
We only allow enough of us to reach the surface
before
plummeting back down.

Can it ever be us saying what we truly mean?
Or do we just not say anything, worshipping the
mediocre?

Are we so afraid of saying "you matter to me"
without
assuming any subtext?

Maybe not...

Devoid of Love

The night falls without a sound,
Cold and alone are we.

The understanding for which you lust
Flares once and then dies.

Devoured by madness,
All hope must end.

Your heart desires no more.
How could you fail to believe?

That our dark emotions surround us, crying:

"Save us from ourselves!"

Stolen Emotion

What have you taken away?
A shadow of misery as memories scream.
Once we enjoyed innocence,
Childlike and untainted.
But then my mind soured

Into a feverish vision of lies.
These thoughts followed after
Your death, after my hate.
Once the love was forgotten.
In a torment of bitterness,
I no longer remember you.

Elizabeth

Signs of love already whispered before you two
met
In a hazily lit hallway on a September morning
As you walked in a single-file line to your room
And the same with her,
Catching her gaze as your classes both passed by

She is the catalyst for anything and everything
that will happen to you
And you'll reminisce long after you've forgotten
about her
Forgetting the name and the face, but never the
essence

Your memories of her sleep throughout your
days
The oldest loves escape under their cover
Whenever you find yourself loving again
The beauties of our imagination turn off our
lives soundlessly
Until we become nothing but flickering lights of
wanting...

I Know a Woman

I know a woman
who is like the final leaf in winter
blowing against the wind.

If you would go near her
during the time of black skies
and talk to her in casual delight
without saying that you love her
or that you will leave her,

Then she will forever be the only
friend you will ever need.

Baltimore Beauty: A Haibun

"I feel like we'll all be dead in about a year anyway."

She liked to say things like that, words that sounded bleak and went up against her carefree, jovial personality. A bit of magic and sunshine personified. But in many ways, she was a woman of numerous contrasts, an enigma that grew more complex with each passing day I knew her. She was from the East Coast yet looked straight out of the campus life I had accustomed myself to in Humboldt, a woman ripped from the past of the late 1960s who enjoyed the tastes of modern music. Curly, strawberry blonde hair, sun-kissed skin, a penchant for bracelets and walking barefoot, she will forever look more "Californian" than I've ever been in all the time I've lived in the state, whatever that might truly mean. Opinionated, but always willing to listen to conflicting views. Constantly unsure of her abilities and what she meant in comparison to her peers, her students, and the work we did, yet consistently proved through her actions to be capable. Memories of love and a desire for friendship and connection

crumpled inside their meaning every time I got
the chance to speak to her. Or more often than
not, failed to say more than a handful of words
before the day would end. The seasons of chance
where we spoke to one another brought in new
combinations of emotions and for that, I shall
always be grateful for being her friend. Students
at the school we worked at almost immediately
christened her with the name Cat and I hope to
think that she changed as much as I did in the
year we worked together.

A cat with sunshine
Turns men back into children
Those are the best days

Gaby

Midnight. She opens the door and
smiles slyly, end of the summer
a faded pink Beauty & the Beast
sweater on, contacts giving
her gray eyes with faint purple
shadow. The leaves outside are
already falling and everyone is
inside because of the heat. Her
mind is on her dog Rocky who
she misses and whether her mother
and father will ever get back
together, how her sister's marriage
is going and when will she
see her brothers again, as she
comes from here to the
Bay Area. Her father's home is
warm with a broken AC.
I love her. Yet I don't know her.
But doesn't love always begin this way?
To truly love someone is to help them.
To mend their soul by lowering your
guard.
I am sitting on the couch right
next to her as she pulls out her
laptop to watch Rick & Morty.

I am just one tiny aspect of her life,
but I love her. As the episode starts,
her childhood home becomes the best
place
I've ever been to; it has food and beer.
She is wrapped around a blanket
with her head on my shoulder. The
wind picks up outside and the
windows are open. She hears her
neighbors shouting, runs out of
battery life and runs into her room
while calling me in. All this time
I was knowing more about her,
taking everything in, every scent
and detail, yet I was still stupid. She
looks at herself in the mirror and runs
through her raven hair. When I first met
her in middle school she dyed it cerulean
blue. She looks at her pile of books
and recommends one to me.
Go Set a Watchman by Harper Lee.
It is no longer warm and now I'm cold.
With the mirror on her desk I see two
of her as she gets out a golden glass pipe
the shape of an elephant. Exhaling,
she is no longer afraid of what
she tells me next.
This is her story...
She whispers it to me and then

the story cuts off. There is a subtle
shift in mood. She soon falls asleep
before I can ask her to elaborate on
what she had just told me. To hear
her familiar, beautiful voice one more time.
She is lively, fun and more depressed than
I will ever be. Why did she tell me
this? I'm nothing to her. I don't know
her life. But then again, what does she
know of me? We've been apart more times
than together but we always seem to drift
back into each other's lives if every briefly.
Like the gentle passing of two streams.
Then I go back into the living room
to sleep on the couch.
The door to her bedroom stays
open the whole time. She mumbles
something in her sleep about a story
she would like to write someday,
something about robots that are created
to look like ancient gods and serve as
representatives of the human race as
they traverse the galaxy. I tell her
that would make a good story,
but she is still asleep. I like to imagine
now that a smile creased her lips.
At 9:00 the next morning we woke up,
I say goodbye, we hug and I drive
back home listening to NPR. It'll

be over a year before I see her again
and almost two years after that. If only...

Serenity

I want to learn how to be a good man
I would also like to be more like a woman
For now, I can only act upon one of them
But in the end, I hope I shape my life like a gem

Lonely and sad is the life that I live
Since no one there is willing to forgive
I reach out my hand to see what I find
Nothing shall escape what is in my mind

Do you believe in me or will you lie?
Because if you do that then I might die
Is changing your mind what you want to do?
I hope it is because there are so few...

Latent Pain

Around, all around, my body shakes.
My dread grows as the stroke of my pen wavers.
It wounds me, and my essence drips
To the wicked pages that are my prison.
In numbness, I fall limply
While nothingness takes my hand.
Now alone my quaking soul falls upon
dead eyes that remind me:

This is your love.

Transformation

Though it is now sour and empty,
Love is still needed, silently but needfully.

Wink like a man torn apart due to vicissitude.
Desire every moment that you need.

How does the cheek not blush over time?
When does Sex happen in bed?

All the kisses feel empty, and so do the smiles.
This rebirth is bound to frighten someone.

Before or after, the Transformation continues.
Yet our fears grow like a knur on a tree.

Fear is a luminous kiss that lies within adversity.
As people are, they go on.

Why do people fight it, to see romance die?
Why do we do it, just to feel good?

Beware! We drove our world to this
Transformation and now it is dead!
Beware! We gave ourselves the freedom
to love, so when did we stumble?

What is marriage after all?
Only adults who wander with a closed heart.

Where is the love then?
Where is the lonely breeze, the descent into
madness?

When do boys become women?
When do girls become men?

Only love is able to decay as time passes.
It is always horrible.

Skin touches skin like the nethermost triumph.
Always crude, lovers smile at one another in
bed.

The next day they embrace, as life goes on.
All of their gestures become painful.

Faces breathe and on them death rises!
Before or after, the Transformation continues.

To lead, we reveal. To reveal, we make.
And God smiles.

How does this not end?
All of the days reveal unpleasant truths.

Sex is a sweet embrace during our time of need.
Yet there is a sizable fear over whether to do it.

Desire, Desire and ever Desire.
Where are we now?

Though Sex is now rough and less pleasurable,
We live, but only for a while.

We perform a rapid descrescendo as we finish.
We have the nerve to asseverate the truth.

The Transformation ends.

Recall the Crazy

My mind is like a thousand women singing
together in symphony.
The music is always frantic and ugly.
I recall how my Mother dreamt and worshipped
As a mad woman soaring and cackling
through a storm.
She would ask the Sky to be less gorgeous
And for it to shine a light above a garden used
for peaches.
Her elaborate language rose to the Moon and
Stars.
Once she was gone They were only friends with
me,
As I desperately search for a purple picture of
you.
Patience recalls love as we lust for life.

In isolation, our desires grow.
As it grows women mourn.
As it festers men become impatient.
As it expands we all suffer.
Beyond this memories begin to echo,
On the bed where the Old Ones speak.
Between our personal meanings of love
and despair we wander,

Amongst the shadows of young lovers.
Life is a journey within static and color.
Above or below the noise, we move on.
We live, but only for a while,
As the devout lead on.

Our memories then turn on us.
The Old Ones join the Young under
a face of anguish.
Lights begin to dim within our minds,
As people from our past join us at all times.
They speak to us sensuously,
As if we were like a child.
People above judge us for our mistakes.
Only then do we finally begin to look for
meaning.
But it is always too late.

A Romance Ballad

I love myself,
And what I hate I must love.
For everyone is just a series of emotions.

I invite you to be my friend.
I want to love everything ... as I weave myself
a tender heart.

Worlds and countries filled with hatred ...
the people are tired of it.
I live within this hatred myself,
and tend to like it.
This hatred may change me,
but I don't want it to.

The Earth is not important ...
it is a tiny piece of the universe ...
it is empty.
It is in my thoughts forever ...
I shall always love it.
Tomorrow I will go to the library and
become one with language.
I am angry that stories are used to justify hate.

The love of my own body.

Punctures, stitches, and knitting ...
cotton, silk, lavender, and thyme.

My depression and anxiety ...
the thinning of my hair ...
the irritated eyes and bent finger.
My allergies to grass and spores,
and of hay and bigots, and of
my own self-loathing,
The heightened sounds in my head ...
voices that make me either super or deaf.
Days of insomnia ... days of frustration ...
light ringing to the ears.
The Cheshire grin as the time left in the day
is reserved for writing,

Is what gets me out of bed each and every
morning.

to the people who say, "I think Pete is gay"

When I was young I never felt comfortable
being around others and at some point, I
began ignoring everyone because I
wanted to be left alone. This is why ...

There had been rumors about me
from when I was six up until I was eighteen
and those kids who started it on that weathered
bus
must have gathered
my thoughts
my feelings
my dreams
into the direction
where I can only
be one thing
and not many.
For twelve years

I knew what they were up to.
They made a reputation mocking me
with what were baseless words.
Words that poisoned my own self
whipped around and controlled me.

Yet I pretended that it would all go away
soon. I was wrong because

Rumors aren't just lies
they are also stories
and most people love a good story
one that gives them control.
Maybe there is some truth
to what they said
but I will never know for sure
until I am ready to say so.

I would like to know who I am

Threads

there
are

threads
connecting

everything and anything
and every thing and any thing
together

beyond
what we see

The Overlook

We reach a spot.
It is high in the mountains
And on the very top.
Looking down upon rising tides.

From there we watch,
The sunny splotch
That is both life and death.

The Beacon

A friendly light comes out to greet me.
I was afraid before, but now I can see.

As the waves roar and crash,
I immediately see our destination to be.

A beacon for me.
For a ship now free,

To explore the narrows
Of the deep blue sea.